DI049589

Tools

Search

Notes

Discuss
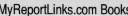
MyReportLinks.com Books

Go!

ENDANGERED AND THREATENED ANIMALS

THE GIANT PANDA

A MyReportLinks.com Book

Carl R. Green

MyReportLinks.com Books

an imprint of

Enslow Publishers, Inc. E

Box 398, 40 Industrial Road
Berkeley Heights, NJ 07922
USA

QL
737
.C214
G7424
2004

MyReportLinks.com Books, an imprint of Enslow Publishers, Inc. MyReportLinks®
is a registered trademark of Enslow Publishers, Inc.

Library of Congress Cataloging-in-Publication Data

Green, Carl R.
  The giant panda / Carl Green.
      p. cm. — (Endangered and threatened animals)
Summary: Describes the physical characteristics, behavior, and habitat
of China's giant pandas, as well as threats to their continued existence
and efforts to save them from extinction.
Includes bibliographical references and index.
  ISBN 0-7660-5061-0
1. Giant panda—Juvenile literature. [1. Giant panda. 2. Pandas. 3.
Endangered species.] I. Title. II. Series.
  QL737.C214G7424 2003
  599.789—dc22

                              2003014396

Printed in the United States of America

10 9 8 7 6 5 4 3 2 1

To Our Readers:
Through the purchase of this book, you and your library gain access to the Report Links that specifically back
up this book.
The Publisher will provide access to the Report Links that back up this book and will keep these Report Links
up to date on **www.myreportlinks.com** for three years from the book's first publication date.
We have done our best to make sure all Internet addresses in this book were active and appropriate when we
went to press. However, the author and the Publisher have no control over, and assume no liability for, the
material available on those Internet sites or on other Web sites they may link to.
The usage of the MyReportLinks.com Books Web site is subject to the terms and conditions stated on the
Usage Policy Statement on **www.myreportlinks.com**.
A password may be required to access the Report Links that back up this book. The password is found on the
bottom of page 4 of this book.
Any comments or suggestions can be sent by e-mail to comments@myreportlinks.com or to the address on
the back cover.

Photo Credits: Athro, Limited, p. 18; ArtToday, pp. 19, 40; AP/Wide World Photos, pp. 11, 13, 27;
Atlanta Fulton County Zoo, Inc., p. 31; BBC News, p. 24; China Daily Information, p. 39; © China
Internet Information Center, pp. 29, 36; © Corel Corporation, pp. 1, 3; © Globio, p. 34; GeoAtlas,
p. 20; Information Please, p. 22; John Bavaro, p. 16; MyReportLinks.com Books, p. 4; National Zoo,
p. 33; Photos.com, pp. 14, 37; U.S. Fish and Wildlife Service, p. 42.

Cover Photo: AP/Wide World Photos.

Contents

MyReportLinks.com Books
Great Books, Great Links, Great for Research!

MyReportLinks.com Books present the information you need to learn about your report subject. In addition, they show you where to go on the Internet for more information. The pre-evaluated Report Links that back up this book are kept up to date on **www.myreportlinks.com**. With the purchase of a MyReportLinks.com Books title, you and your library gain access to the Report Links that specifically back up that book. The Report Links save hours of research time and link to dozens—even hundreds—of Web sites, source documents, and photos related to your report topic.

Please see "To Our Readers" on the Copyright page for important information about this book, the MyReportLinks.com Books Web site, and the Report Links that back up this book.

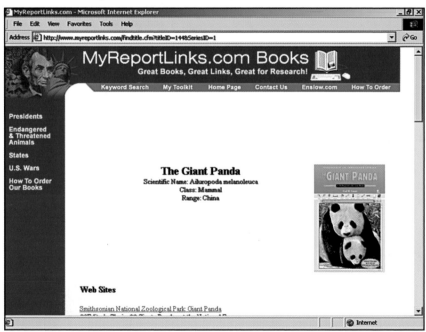

Access:

The Publisher will provide access to the Report Links that back up this book and will try to keep these Report Links up to date on our Web site for three years from the book's first publication date. Please enter **EGP4425** if asked for a password.

Report Links

The Internet sites described below can be accessed at
http://www.myreportlinks.com

Editor's choice

▶**Smithsonian National Zoological Park: Giant Panda**
The Smithsonian National Zoological Park is the home of giant pandas
Mei Xiang and Tian Tian. You can look at the pandas on Web cams,
learn about their habitat, and find out more about the National Zoo.
News, facts, and other information about pandas can also be found.

　　　　　　　Link to this Internet site from http://www.myreportlinks.com

Editor's choice

▶**Animal Info—Giant Panda**
This page contains facts, figures, and photographs of the giant
panda. Here you will find information about the panda's physical
characteristics, status, biology, and habitat. A comprehensive
list of resources is included.

　　　　　　　Link to this Internet site from http://www.myreportlinks.com

Editor's choice

▶**Zoological Society of San Diego: Panda Central**
The world famous San Diego Zoo is home to giant pandas Bai Yun,
Gao Gao, and Hua Mei. This site is loaded with panda facts, news,
videos, and photographs.

　　　　　　　Link to this Internet site from http://www.myreportlinks.com

Editor's choice

▶**Flagship Species: Giant Panda**
The World Wildlife Fund has worked for over forty years to conserve
endangered species and their threatened habitats. Here you can learn
about the giant panda, the threats to its existence, and what the WWF
is doing to help.

　　　　　　　Link to this Internet site from http://www.myreportlinks.com

Editor's choice

▶**About the Giant Panda**
This site from China Daily is dedicated to the giant panda. Here
you will learn about the panda's physical characteristics, diet, mating,
habitat, and preservation. A number of news articles and photographs
are also included.

　　　　　　　Link to this Internet site from http://www.myreportlinks.com

Editor's choice

▶**Giant Panda**
Defenders of Wildlife have designed this site to help you learn about
the panda's physical characteristics, habitat, behavior patterns, declining
numbers, and more.

　　　　　　　Link to this Internet site from http://www.myreportlinks.com

Report Links

 The Internet sites described below can be accessed at
http://www.myreportlinks.com

▶ *Ailuropoda melanoleuca*
This site from University of Michigan's Animal Diversity Web contains a
wealth of panda facts. Here you will learn about the panda's natural history,
distribution, classification, and conservation biology.

Link to this Internet site from http://www.myreportlinks.com

▶ **American Bamboo: General Bamboo Information**
The giant panda's diet consists of 99 percent bamboo. Here you will find
information about the different types of bamboo, where they are found,
how they are used, and everything else that you may want to know about
this useful grass.

Link to this Internet site from http://www.myreportlinks.com

▶ **Animal Planet: Meet the Pandas**
Here you will meet the National Zoo's pandas, Mei Xiang and Tian Tian.
You will learn about the pandas, their Chinese home, their voyage to America,
their keepers, and species facts. Photographs, videos, and an interactive section
are included.

Link to this Internet site from http://www.myreportlinks.com

▶ **BBC News: Cold War Peace Panda Dies**
Hsing-Hsing and his partner, Ling Ling, were a gift from China to the
United States in 1972. The pair of pandas soon found a home at the
Smithsonian National Zoo. This site features an article about the life and
death of Hsing-Hsing.

Link to this Internet site from http://www.myreportlinks.com

▶ **Chengdu Research Base of Giant Panda Breeding**
The Chengdu Zoo and Chengdu Research Base of Giant Panda Breeding have
spent half of a century helping to ensure the survival of the giant panda. Here
you will learn about the organization, its genetic and reproductive research,
tourist information, news, panda facts, and much more.

Link to this Internet site from http://www.myreportlinks.com

▶ **China in Brief**
China is the home of the Giant Panda. This official Web site from the People's
Republic of China provides an overview of the country's culture. Here you
will find information about Chinese history, geography, government, art,
religion, and more.

Link to this Internet site from http://www.myreportlinks.com

Any comments? Contact us: **comments@myreportlinks.com**

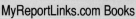
Report Links

The Internet sites described below can be accessed at http://www.myreportlinks.com

▶ **Endangered!: Giant Panda**
This site from the American Museum of Natural History describes the panda's slide toward endangerment. The tale is illustrated by panda distribution maps and photographs. You will also learn about the other creatures that share the Wolong Reserve with the giant panda.

Link to this Internet site from http://www.myreportlinks.com

▶ **Endangered Species: Pandas**
This site from the World Wildlife Fund is dedicated to the giant panda. Here you will find panda facts, news, conservation information, a slide show, a pop quiz, and more!

Link to this Internet site from http://www.myreportlinks.com

▶ **Endangered Species Act of 1973**
The United States House of Representatives Committee on Resources Web site contains the complete text of the Endangered Species Act of 1973.

Link to this Internet site from http://www.myreportlinks.com

▶ **Female Explorers: A Time for Loving**
In 1936, during a visit to China, American fashion designer Ruth Harkness found a baby giant panda named Su-Lin. Thanks to Harkness, Su-Lin became the first panda seen in the United States. This site tells the full story of America's love of Su-Lin.

Link to this Internet site from http://www.myreportlinks.com

▶ **Georgia's Panda Project**
At Zoo Atlanta's Web site you will learn about pandas, their environment, threats to their survival, and conservation efforts. The legend of how the pandas got their markings is also included. Do not forget to check out the zoo's "Giant Panda Live Cam."

Link to this Internet site from http://www.myreportlinks.com

▶ **Giant Panda**
This Web site from the China Internet Information Center contains giant panda news, pictures, and facts. Information about legislation and conservation efforts relating to the panda can also be found here.

Link to this Internet site from http://www.myreportlinks.com

Report Links

The Internet sites described below can be accessed at
http://www.myreportlinks.com

▶**Giant Panda**
This site provides the basic facts about the giant panda. Read a description of
the panda and its habitat, diet, and more.

Link to this Internet site from http://www.myreportlinks.com

▶**Giant Panda Conservation Plan**
Learn about past and current panda conservation attempts and their effects
in this article from the American Zoo and Aquarium Association. Click on
"Pandas in the Public Eye" to find out how famous zoo pandas are
instrumental in ongoing efforts to save their species.

Link to this Internet site from http://www.myreportlinks.com

▶**Homeland of Giant Panda**
4panda.com offers tours of the giant panda's environment. Here you will learn
about giant pandas, their distribution, threats, conservation, and reproduction.
Profiles of Chengdu Zoo, Wolong Panda Reserve, and other important panda
sites are also included.

Link to this Internet site from http://www.myreportlinks.com

▶**The Hong Kong Center for Panda Conservation**
The Hong Kong Center for Panda Conservation is dedicated to saving the
giant panda. Here you will learn panda facts and read the latest panda news.
You can also play panda games.

Link to this Internet site from http://www.myreportlinks.com

▶**Ministry of Foreign Affairs of the People's Republic of China**
This outline from the Information Office of the State Council of the People's
Republic of China explains what the government is doing to protect the
panda's environment. You will learn about governmental organizations and
the roles they play in trying to save the panda.

Link to this Internet site from http://www.myreportlinks.com

▶**Nixon's China Game**
Giant pandas Hsing-Hsing and Ling Ling were gifts to the United States from
the Chinese government in 1972. They were a symbol of a new era of peaceful
relations between the two countries. Here you will learn about President
Richard Nixon's historic visit to China.

Link to this Internet site from http://www.myreportlinks.com

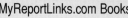

Report Links

 The Internet sites described below can be accessed at
http://www.myreportlinks.com

▶**Panda Babies Offer Hope**
On this site from FactMonster.com, you can read an article about eight
baby pandas that were born in China's Wolong Panda Reserve.

Link to this Internet site from http://www.myreportlinks.com

▶**Panda Habitat Research in China**
Scientists at Michigan State University are documenting information
about how people affect the giant panda's fragile habitat. This site
features updates, stories, and videos from the school's team in the
Wolong Panda Nature Reserve in southwestern China.

Link to this Internet site from http://www.myreportlinks.com

▶**The Panda's Thumb**
Pandas use an enlarged wrist bone as a thumb with which they grasp
bamboo. Here you will learn about the panda's unusual "pseudo-
thumb" and the debate revolving around its evolutionary meaning.

Link to this Internet site from http://www.myreportlinks.com

▶**PBS Nature: The Panda Baby**
Here you will learn about the survival of Hua Mei, the San Diego Zoo's
baby panda, what zoos are doing to save pandas, the first panda to be
displayed in the United States, and much more.

Link to this Internet site from http://www.myreportlinks.com

▶***Science News*: The Lives of Pandas**
This article from *Science News* is about the life, birth, and diet of the
giant panda. A diagram and description of the panda's thumb-like paw
pad is included.

Link to this Internet site from http://www.myreportlinks.com

▶**Wolong Giant Panda Reserve**
The Wolong Nature Reserve provides the giant panda with its best
chance for survival in its native habitat. Here you will learn about the
reserve's history and how it operates. Field updates, rescues, and releases
are also documented here.

Link to this Internet site from http://www.myreportlinks.com

Giant Panda Facts

Scientific Name	*Ailuropoda melanoleuca.* The Chinese call the giant panda *da xiong mao* (dah-shong mah-oo)—the "large cat-bear."
Closest Relatives	The giant panda is most often classified as a member of *Ursidae*—the bears. As a bear, its closest relative is the South American spectacled bear. Other scientists argue that the giant panda is a member of *Procyonidae*—the raccoons. In that family, its closest relative would be the red panda.
Current Habitat	All wild giant pandas live in the dense bamboo forests of the mountains of western China.

Size and Weight	Average	*Adult male*	*Adult female*
	Length:	4 to 6 ft. (1.2 to 1.8 m)	3.5 to 4.5 ft.(1.1 to 1.4 m)
	Height:	27 to 32 in. (69 to 81 cm)	24 to 30 in. (61 to 76 cm)
	Weight:	230 lbs. (104 kg)	198 lbs. (89.8 kg)

Diet	Giant pandas feed on the shoots, leaves, and stems of the bamboo. In one year, an adult panda can consume more than ten thousand pounds of bamboo. On occasion, pandas also eat fish, small rodents, honey, and flowering plants.
Current Populations	Estimates place the wild population of giant pandas at between 700 and 1,200. Another 140 live in zoos and breeding centers.
Special Adaptations	The giant panda uses a thumb-like wrist bone to grasp bamboo stalks. Its thick, dense coat protects it from cold, snow, and rain at altitudes as high as 10,500 feet (3,200 m).
Life Span	In the wild: about 20–22 years. In captivity: up to 30 years.
Vocalizations	Giant pandas have a large "vocabulary." They chirp during mating, honk in times of stress, and bark or click their teeth to frighten enemies. A squeal signals submission or pain, and a bleating, goat-like sound indicates a friendly contact.
Main Threats	Habitat destruction, poaching, periodic die-offs of bamboo, and loss of genetic diversity.
Legislative Status	In the United States, pandas are protected by the Endangered Species Act of 1973. Zoos that want to import pandas must follow strict rules laid down by the Fish and Wildlife Service. China created the first of its giant panda reserves in 1963.
Organizations Working to Save the Panda	• Center for Reproduction of Endangered Species • China Wildlife Conservation Organization • North American Giant Panda Conservation Foundation; World Wildlife Fund • Zoological Society of San Diego; Zoo Atlanta; National Zoological Park; Memphis Zoo

All figures are estimates.

Ailuropoda melanoleuca

Animal lovers watch in awe as a Bengal tiger paces around its cage. Not far away, children giggle as young chimpanzees play a rough-and-tumble game of tag. Farther down the line, an elephant uncurls its trunk and sprays the crowd with water. Surely, this is a normal day at the zoo.

As it turns out, this is far from being a normal day. The zoo has just welcomed some new guests. Follow the surging crowd to the enclosure where *Ailuropoda melanoleuca* lives. There is the zoo's new star, calmly munching a bamboo stalk. Someone whispers, "She's a real, live black-and-white teddy bear!" You do not need a sign to tell you that you are face-to-face with China's best-loved visitor—the giant panda.

If they are not ▶ feeding or looking for food, pandas are usually resting.

▶ Hearts Go Out to the Panda

Why do people adore the giant panda? Scientists believe the answer lies in the panda's nonthreatening looks. Like toddlers, pandas have large heads and round, flat faces. Also like babies, their bodies give the illusion of being soft and cuddly. Even the panda's eyes look big and gentle, thanks to its black eye patches.[1]

Of course, giant pandas are ten times the size of a human baby. Even so, these slow-moving bamboo eaters inspire joy, not fear. Watch a panda at play. You cannot help but smile to see it turn clumsy somersaults. If a soccer ball is thrown into the pen, the panda will likely play a lively game—until its sharp claws rip the ball to shreds.[2]

A zookeeper answers questions about the giant panda. Her listeners look upset when she confirms that the species is in danger of extinction. Unlike animals such as snail darters and crested toads, people deeply care about pandas. That fact led the World Wildlife Fund (WWF) to pick the giant panda as its symbol. Today, a black-and-white panda logo carries the WWF's conservation message across the globe.

▶ Legend of the Giant Panda

There are many stories about how the panda got its patches of black fur. An old Tibetan legend tells us that pandas once were as white as polar bears. In that long-ago time, a panda cub played with a flock of sheep tended by four sisters. One day a leopard sprang at the cub. The sisters grabbed their shepherd's crooks and tried to chase the predator away. In the confusion, the cub escaped. The angry leopard turned on the girls and killed them.

All of China's giant pandas came to the funeral. As a sign of their grief, they wore black armbands. When they hugged and cried and wiped their eyes, their tears caused the dye in the armbands to run. Each hug and pat left a black splotch on their white fur. When they saw what had happened, the pandas vowed never to wash off the black markings. Later, the pandas turned the girls' graves into a mountain with four tall peaks. The mountain still stands in Sichuan Province near the Wolong Nature Reserve. Villagers call it *Siguniang*—the Four Sisters Mountain.[3]

 Chinese philosophy, art, and science are all affected by the concept of yin and yang. This relates to the ideal of opposites living together in perfect harmony. The panda is considered a living example of yin and yang because it is so comfortable in its coat of black-and-white fur.

▶ A Complex Family Tree

Scientists long have wondered, "Is the giant panda a bear or a raccoon?" The ancient Chinese thought the panda looked like a bear, so they called it a bear. One of their many names for the panda was *zhu xiong,* the "bamboo bear." When modern naturalists arrived on the scene, most agreed with the old name. It seemed logical to put the giant panda in the bear family—the *Ursidae.* Others shook their heads. The giant panda, they argued, is more like the smaller, raccoon-like red panda. In their minds, giant pandas belong in the raccoon family—the *Procyonidae.*[4]

▲ Although the red panda has similar facial features to that of the giant panda, they are not closely related. The giant panda is considered part of the bear family, whereas the red panda is thought to belong to the raccoon family.

Each side gathered data to prove its case. The pro-raccoon side argued that the teeth, skulls, and forepaws of giant pandas and red pandas are very much alike in size and the way they act. Both species eat bamboo. Both have similar facial markings. The people who thought it was more like a bear claimed that size and shape *do* count. Newborn bears and newborn giant pandas are much alike. As adults, pandas have big, round bear-like bodies. Their rounded ears are shaped like those of the Asiatic black bear. A red panda, by contrast, has pointed ears.

Lab work furnished the tiebreaker. Tests showed that the giant panda's blood and genetic background are more bear-like than raccoon-like. Based on those results, textbooks assigned giant pandas to the bear family—on a branch of their own. Red pandas are given their own branch in the raccoon family. Fossils prove that the two pandas shared a common ancestor, but each went its own way millions of years ago. The giant panda's closest modern relative is the South American spectacled bear.[5]

This long-running debate does not interest the giant panda. These animals spend their days eating and sleeping. They do not worry, scientist Edwin Colbert wrote in 1938, about the quarrels they cause just by being themselves.[6]

Chapter 2

A Lonely Life on a Bamboo Mountain

Snow flurries drift across the bright winter sky. High on a mountain ridge, a sharp snap echoes in the still air. Hidden in a grove of swaying bamboo, a giant panda sniffs at a slender stalk. When she is sure the bamboo is good to eat, she chomps it down like a stalk of celery after stripping away the outer layers. At last, hunger eased, she sits back. It is time for a morning nap. Within a circle of three thousand feet (914 m) lay all that the female needs. She has bamboo to eat and a mate ranging nearby. A few yards away is the hollow tree where she someday will give birth.[1]

Thick coat of black and white provides warmth and may provide camouflage

White fur on back

Black fur in the shoulder area

5-inch-long tail

Black around eyes

Large molars, strong jaw for crunching tough bamboo

Forepaw has elongated wrist bone and sixth finger; helps in gripping bamboo stalks

At Home in the Mountains

Six-month-old cubs born and raised in a zoo are quite friendly and huggable. The adults are quite a different matter. Pandas look soft and playful, but they are bear-like in shape and temper. Those sharp claws and teeth have mauled a number of unlucky or unwise zookeepers.

As bears go, giant pandas are on the small side. Females weigh in at around 200 pounds (91 kg) and measure 24 to 30 inches (61–76 cm) at the shoulder. Mature males are 10 to 20 percent larger, tipping the scales at 230 pounds (104 kg) or more. If a big male panda could stand fully erect, he would look a six-foot man in the eye.[2]

Naturalists admire the giant panda's striking black-and-white coat. The thick, oily fur protects its owner from winter cold and summer rains. Scientists guess that the panda's coat also serves as camouflage. Seen against a rocky, snow-covered hillside, the panda nearly vanishes from view. Other scientists think the panda's distinctive black and white coat lets pandas spot one another.[3] The bold markings might also serve as a warning to predators.

The giant panda's life is tied tightly to bamboo. It has poor eyesight, but its keen sense of smell helps it pick out the choicest shoots and stems called *culms*. Nature has equipped its forepaws with what look like thumbs for grasping the tough stems and leaves. Each "thumb" is an enlarged wrist bone covered with a fleshy pad of skin. As it feeds, the panda's strong jaws and large molars crush the tough bamboo stalks. Splinters that would choke most animals slide down its leathery and mucous-lined throat.

Bamboo makes up 99 percent of the giant panda's diet. Even so, its digestive system is a holdover from an age when they ate meat, not plants. The panda's intestine,

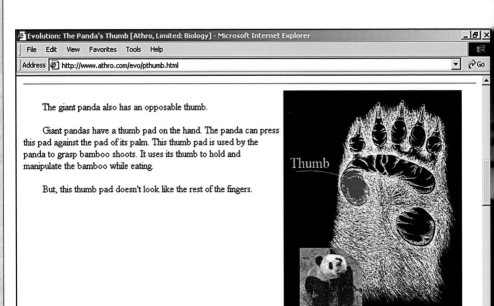

Evolution: The Panda's Thumb [Athro, Limited: Biology] - Microsoft Internet Explorer

File   Edit   View   Favorites   Tools   Help

Address http://www.athro.com/evo/pthumb.html   Go

The giant panda also has an opposable thumb.

Giant pandas have a thumb pad on the hand. The panda can press this pad against the pad of its palm. This thumb pad is used by the panda to grasp bamboo shoots. It uses its thumb to hold and manipulate the bamboo while eating.

But, this thumb pad doesn't look like the rest of the fingers.

Thumb

The panda's thumb pad. Modified from *Davis, 1964*.

Look carefully at the bones in the giant panda's hand. Inside the thumb pad is the blue "thumb" bone. Does it look the same as the rest of the panda's

"Thumb"

Internet

▲ Pandas eat bamboo. They hold the bamboo between their fingers and "thumbs." However, because it is merely an enlarged portion of its wrist bone, the panda's thumb is only capable of slight movement.

where digestion takes place, is only five to seven times its body length. By contrast, a cow's intestine measures twenty times its body length. As a result, the panda can digest only 20 percent of the bamboo's food value. A cow retains some 60 percent of the nutrients in the hay it eats.

Giant pandas must eat massive amounts of bamboo to get enough nutrition. Adults need up to forty pounds (18 kg) of leaves and culms a day. If they are feeding on fresh shoots, their day's intake doubles to around eighty pounds (36 kg).[4] Because this diet contains little fat, pandas do not hibernate. They would starve if they tried to sleep the winter away in a den.

▷ A Mountain Habitat

Giant pandas once roamed the mountains of Burma (now called Myanmar), Laos, Vietnam, and China. Today, human settlement has reduced the panda's territory to a handful of wildlife reserves. All can be found in the rugged mountains of western China, mainly in Sichuan Province. The upland ridges are often covered in thick clouds and pelted by heavy rains and snowstorms.

The arrow and umbrella bamboos favored by giant pandas thrive at altitudes of five thousand to twelve thousand feet (3,658 m). Shaded by taller trees, the fast-growing stalks cluster in thick groves. One study counted one million bamboo culms per square mile. A grove of that size can support as many as five giant pandas.[5] Thanks to their high water content, the plants also supply much of the water that pandas need.

▲ Pandas eat sitting upright so that their front paws can grasp the bamboo. Their powerful jaws and teeth allow them to bite off and chew small pieces of the tough stalks.

Pandas share their misty habitat with many plants and animals. In a single reserve, naturalists counted over four thousand species of native plants. Nine species of pheasant build their nests in the mountains of Sichuan. The region's mammals include golden monkeys, porcupines, and deer.[6] Leopards, weasels, and packs of wild dogs known as *dholes* prey on unguarded panda cubs. All of these predators scatter when an angry mother panda lumbers to the rescue.

Keeping To Themselves

Giant pandas shy away from contact with other animals— even other pandas. They seem content to spend quiet days feeding and resting. Even this low level of activity requires

▲ Pandas are native to central China.

vast amounts of bamboo. Panda expert George Schaller's studies show that a panda spends up to twelve hours a day feeding. Up at dawn, the panda stuffs its stomach full of leaves, stems, and shoots. Full at last, it rests for two to four hours. Then, hungry again, it repeats the routine. As the day drifts past, the panda takes time to groom its fur and mark nearby trees with its scent.[7]

In the spring, the giant panda's lifestyle changes abruptly. For a brief two or three weeks, females come into heat. Nearby males respond to their calls and scent marks. Naturalists believe that these strong-smelling smears give clues to their maker's sex, identity, and intentions.[8] If the male is interested, he lets loose a chorus of moans, hoots, yips, and barks. Drawn by his calls, the female seeks him out. The two must mate during the two to five days when she can become pregnant.[9] Afterward, the female returns to her own range. In most cases, the male never sees the cub he has fathered.

The female makes her den in a hollow tree. She will carry the unborn cub for 97 to 165 days. Almost all growth takes place during the last 45 to 60 days. This delay, scientists believe, allows the cub to be born when food is most plentiful. The brief growth period produces cubs that are born blind, helpless, and nearly naked. A typical cub weighs only three or four ounces (85 to 113 g). Twin births are common, but the weaker cub almost always dies. Nursed by a loving mother, the surviving cub grows quickly. By three weeks it weighs a robust two pounds (.9 kg). More and more, it looks like a small copy of the female.[10]

The cub stays close to its mother for up to two years. During these months she teaches it the skills it will need as an adult. By five months, the cub is strong enough to travel by her side. As weeks and months pass, it learns to

feed on the bamboo that will be its adult diet. Weaning begins, and by its first birthday, nursing gradually reduces. A year later, the female comes in heat again. She drives the cub away and begins a new mating cycle. The two-year-old now weighs a hundred pounds or more. Slowly it drifts away to find its own range. By age six, the cub will be sexually mature and ready to seek its own mate.

This two-year cycle limits the number of cubs a female can raise. At best, she will give birth to only four or five cubs during her twenty-year lifetime. Of those five, only two are likely to survive. Food shortages, poachers, disease, and habitat loss are pushing giant pandas ever closer to extinction.[11]

▲ These newborn pandas will not be able to open their eyes for six to eight weeks. They will not move around by themselves until three months after birth and will nurse for about a year.

Chapter 3

Threats to the Giant Panda's Survival

In March 1983, a Chinese farmer stood before the judge, his head bowed. Leng Zhizhong was accused of poaching, a common crime in the Wolong Natural Reserve. He told the judge that he had not meant to kill the rare animal that he had snared. His only thought had been to trap a male musk deer. If the plan had worked, he would have sold the musk gland to a perfume maker. "I am poor," Zhizhong said, "and did it to help my family."

After hearing from both sides, the judge read his verdict: "The sentence is two years in prison," he told the poacher.

Today's punishments are far more severe. China's courts have sentenced a number of poachers to life in prison. A few have been condemned to death. In every case, the crime was the same: Each man had killed one or more giant pandas.[1]

▶ Nature Can Be a Threat, Too

Wildlife lovers cheer any action that protects the giant panda. They worry that the number of wild pandas may have dipped as low as seven hundred. A more hopeful count puts the number at 1,200 or so. The threats that have been killing off the panda are both natural and human-made.

Life in the wild has always been full of hazards. Newborn cubs, left alone while their mothers are feeding, are easy prey for weasels. Older cubs fall victim to leopards or packs of dholes. A panda that stops eating may be fighting a different kind of killer. Roundworms stop growth and sap their host's

energy. Even when it is sick, a panda seldom acts the part. Doing so would invite attack by hungry predators.[2]

In 1983, searchers found the bodies of sixty-two giant pandas in China's Qionglai Mountains. Neither poachers nor predators were to blame. The pandas starved to death after a mass die-off of arrow bamboo. Naturalists warn that die-offs are part of bamboo's life cycle. Within a region, all the plants of a bamboo species produce flowers, go to seed, and then die at the same time. The seeds will sprout, but new plants take years to mature. Depending on the species, the time between die-offs ranges from 3 to 120 years.[3]

There are many reasons why the panda is endangered. Some of these include bamboo die-off, slow reproductive rates, and poaching. Recent studies tell us that there may be less than a thousand giant pandas living in the wild and in captivity.

In ancient times, a hungry giant panda could move to a new habitat. Today, migration is not always an option. Roads, train tracks, farms, and villages have pushed high into the mountains. Pandas hate to move in the best of times. Now, wary of man-made obstacles, they give up the search for new feeding areas. One by one, the stranded pandas will die of hunger as the bamboo dies off.

Man-Made Threats

George Schaller believes that die-offs and other natural threats can be managed. The greatest peril, he says, comes from poachers.[4] These illegal hunters risk their lives in hopes of scoring big payoffs. Some trap young pandas and try to sell them to zoos and private collectors. Others kill and skin adult pandas. Shady dealers pay up to four thousand dollars for a good pelt. The dealers then smuggle the pelts into Japan, Taiwan, or Hong Kong. Sold on the black market, a good pelt brings ten thousand dollars or more. As one poacher told police, "If you hadn't caught me, I would have been rich."[5]

China passed a tough wildlife protection law in 1989. The law forbids the capture, killing, or trading of any protected species. Stiffer penalties and improved policing help, but they have not put a stop to poaching. In 1990, a WWF agent proved that fact by posing as a buyer from Taiwan. As she toured China, a dealer tried to sell her two live cubs for $112,000. At other stops, she found sixteen panda pelts for sale.[6]

Tree cutting is the primary risk to the giant panda. Once the trees are cut, bamboo stops growing and rain erodes the soil. Logging is forbidden in China's reserves, but villagers believe the forests are there to use. Firewood is costly, and many villagers are too poor to buy it. Friendly

guards sometimes look the other way when they see trees being cut. In a few cases, armed woodcutters have opened fire when guards did try to stop them.[7]

Tourists who come to see wild pandas add another type of stress. The visitors create jobs in remote areas, but the cost is high. City folk demand smooth roads, soft beds, and extra helpings of Wolong's famous smoked pork. Caring for their needs often pollutes the woods and streams. If well managed, the dollars spent by tourists can help pay for conservation measures. When tourism surges out of control, however, wildlife is the big loser.[8]

▶ The Greatest Threat: Loss of Habitat

The story dates back to an age when humans first learned the art of farming. Early farmers planted the fertile plains and valleys. Later, with ever more mouths to feed, they pushed into the uplands. Along the way they cut trees for fuel and lumber and hunted animals for meat and fur. Their herds overgrazed the hillsides. With forest cover lost, rain washed away the topsoil.[9]

William Sheldon saw the results when he toured China in the 1930s. "Even at two thousand feet above the river bottom," he wrote, " . . . every possible acre of earth seemed planted with corn." As he pushed higher, Sheldon saw that entire hillsides were without trees. The sight, he noted, "has been very depressing."[10] As farming advanced, the giant pandas retreated. By Sheldon's day, the bamboo bears were confined to the mountains of western China.

Today, China must feed, clothe, and house over 1.2 billion people. Despite increasing population pressures, the government is doing its best to safeguard wild habitat. The losses, however, continue to mount. Between the mid-1970s and the mid-1980s, the panda lost 50 percent of its remaining habitat. Demand for cheap products made in China causes the country to use up more of its natural resources. If knit together, Wolong and the other reserves would cover only 5,021 square miles (13,004 km^2). North America's Greater Yellowstone Ecosystem is four times that size.[11]

The plight of the 500,000-acre Wolong reserve spotlights the problem. Satellite photos made in the early 1970s show the area losing 52 acres of wildlife habitat per year. After the park was created in 1975, panda habitat

Hua Mei, the fifth giant panda born in the United States, was welcomed to the San Diego Zoo on August 21, 1999. This photo was taken when she was sixteen weeks old. Her mother, Bai Yun, is on a twelve-year reproductive loan that started in 1996.

vanished at four times that rate—237 acres a year. Wolong's panda population is dropping almost as quickly. Naturalists counted 145 giant pandas there in 1974. In 1986, the count dipped to 72.[12]

As more habitat is nibbled away, giant panda populations become more separated from each other. Small populations become inbred and lose genetic diversity. This results in lower fertility and more stillborn cubs. Should the climate change, the survivors will find it harder to adapt. Today, only three reserves support enough pandas to keep inbreeding from becoming a threat. In reserves with as few as twenty pandas, the problem already exists.[13]

▶ Use Everything!

Villagers who share the giant panda's habitat mean no harm to their furry neighbors. Saving wildlife, however, takes a backseat when children are cold and hungry. Writer Vaclav Smil spoke to a peasant farmer who argued that the land is there to be used. "If there's a mountain, we'll cover it with wheat," the man said. "If there's water to be found, we'll use it all to plant rice."[14]

The challenge is clear. If the world wants to save the giant panda, there is work to be done . . . and soon.

Save the Giant Panda!

In ancient times, Chinese rulers regarded the giant panda with awe. Only honored guests were given panda pelts as gifts. News of the rare "white bears" did not reach the outside world until 1869. That was the year a French missionary sent the first panda skins back to Europe. In a letter to his son, Père Armand David said the giant panda

▲ Although young giant pandas sometimes are seen resting on tree limbs, they usually are found on the ground. For shelter, they prefer caves, hollow trees, and rock crevices.

was "the prettiest kind of animal I know. . . . Perhaps it is new to science!"[1]

As word of the white bear spread, big-game hunters took up the chase. Each wanted to be the first westerner to kill a giant panda. Theodore Roosevelt, Jr., and his brother Kermit were the first. In 1929, they journeyed to China in pursuit of the giant panda. Like their president father, they saw hunting as a grand sport. In the western mountains, guides led them to a panda sleeping in a tree. Both men fired, and the hapless panda fell at their feet.

In 1936, Ruth Harkness set out to complete her late husband's quest. His dream had been to capture a live cub. The trip led the American fashion designer deep into China's bamboo forests. After guides frightened away a mother panda, Harkness pulled a three-pound (1.4 kg) cub from its den. She nursed it from a bottle and named it Su-Lin. Back in the United States, "panda-monium" broke out.[2] Chicago's Brookfield Zoo soon bought Su Lin. The zoo had its biggest influx of visitors the day the panda went on display.

▶ An Action Plan Develops

After World War II, naturalists trekked to China to study the giant panda. As they learned more about the species, a hard truth surfaced. Loss of habitat was putting the panda at risk. If the world did not act, the panda would be lost.

Governments joined hands in the 1970s to protect endangered wildlife. In the United States, Congress passed the 1973 Endangered Species Act. That same year, over one hundred nations signed the Convention on International Trade in Endangered Species (CITES). The goal was to end the trade in rare animals and animal parts.

By the 1990s, the numbers showed that the drive to save the panda was falling short. China, with backing by the WWF, the United States, and other nations, adopted a "Panda Management Plan." The plan lists six main goals:

- Construct more nature reserves with giant panda habitats.

- Establish safe areas between panda populations for pandas to travel between.

- Reduce poaching by doing a better job of guarding the reserves.

- Improve the rural way of life. When their lives get better, villagers are less likely to plunder the reserves for food, furs, and fuel.

▲ Zoo Atlanta is just one place that has begun a captive breeding program for the giant panda.

- Strengthen efforts to train villagers in the need to protect the environment.

- Use captive breeding programs to find ways to improve the birth rate of wild pandas.[3] Captive breeding programs focus on efforts to increase the number of live births of captive members of an endangered species.

▶ Captive Breeding Programs

Naturalists prefer to leave endangered animals free to live and breed in the wild. Giant pandas are an exception. At the best of times, a female raises only a few cubs during her lifetime. Today, with so few pandas left, wild pandas are hard-pressed to maintain their numbers. The answer may lie in captive breeding programs.

Some captive animals, such as the Bengal tiger, mate readily. The giant panda is not one of them. Only through trial and error have scientists found ways to increase panda birthrates. The first success came in 1963 with the birth of a cub at the Beijing Zoo. The first live birth outside of China came at the Mexico City Zoo in 1980. Since then, Mexico's pandas have produced seven more cubs. Five lived to become adults. This success rate is a far cry from the days when most zoo-born cubs died.[4]

Don Lindburg leads the giant panda team at the San Diego Zoo. In a 2002 State of the Panda report, he praised the Wolong breeding program. "There have been two spectacular results," Lindburg says. "First, the pregnancy rate is up—way up! Second, infant survival has [greatly] improved." He credits the change to better feeding, health care, housing, and improved handling of cubs. Even at Wolong, females who give birth to twins often abandon one of them. Thanks to better formulas and bottles, the center's nursemaids are saving those cubs. "In the last two years

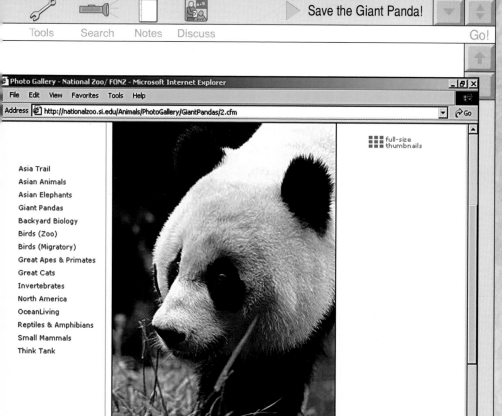

Photo Gallery - National Zoo/ FONZ - Microsoft Internet Explorer

File   Edit   View   Favorites   Tools   Help

Address http://nationalzoo.si.edu/Animals/PhotoGallery/GiantPandas/2.cfm   Go

full-size
thumbnails

Asia Trail
Asian Animals
Asian Elephants
Giant Pandas
Backyard Biology
Birds (Zoo)
Birds (Migratory)
Great Apes & Primates
Great Cats
Invertebrates
North America
OceanLiving
Reptiles & Amphibians
Small Mammals
Think Tank

Internet

China is dedicated to preserving the giant panda. To protect the species from poachers and other threats, the Chinese government has established twenty-seven nature reserves and breeding programs in thirty-two zoos.

[at Wolong]," Lindburg reports, "seventeen of eighteen mother-reared and nursery-reared panda cubs survived."[5]

All too often, captive males show little interest in mating. Doctors have tackled the problem by using artificial insemination. When the female is ready to conceive, they put her to sleep. Then they implant sperm drawn from a healthy male. The first success using this technique came at the Beijing Zoo in 1978. The process also allows breeders to improve genetic diversity. In 1982, sperm taken from a male in London was flown to Spain. There it was used to conceive a healthy cub. Scientists now are looking

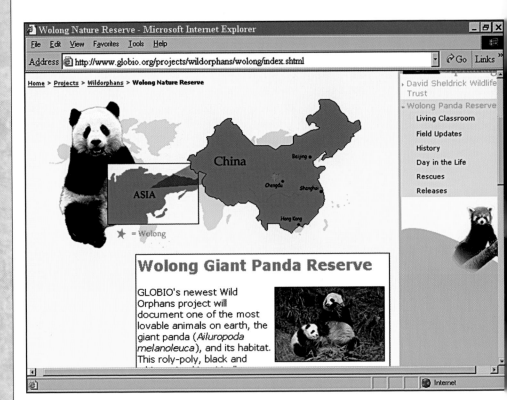

The Wolong Nature Reserve cares for pandas in the mountains of China's Sichuan Province. Naturalists are working there to save the giant panda through research into panda breeding and bamboo ecology.

ahead to the day when they welcome the first "test-tube" cub into the world.[6]

▶ A Visit to Wolong Nature Reserve

Wolong Nature Reserve is one of the keys to the giant panda's future. To reach the reserve, visitors follow bumpy dirt roads that climb into the Qionglai Mountains. China's crowded cities fall behind. Viewing Wolong for the first time, one visitor was awestruck. She described the site as "the most beautiful place I've ever been."[7]

Wolong meets all of the giant panda's needs. Seven types of bamboo grow on quiet hillsides. Clear streams flow past groves of tall trees. Guards patrol the reserve to enforce the "five nos." The local farmers know this to mean: no fire, no cutting trees, no hunting, no plowing, and no damaging forest regrowth.[8] With help from the WWF, the breeding center has been upgraded. The pandas kept there for study and breeding live in roomy enclosures. Pandas destined for release move to larger pens that duplicate Wolong's wild habitat.

Much time, money, and love have flowed into the Wolong project. Even so, storm clouds hover over the reserve. In just twenty years, the human population has increased by 70 percent. The change has led to more land being cleared. Deep in the forest, more snares are being set. As settlements edge higher into the hills, pandas retreat farther up the mountain. Should a bamboo die-off occur, the Wolong pandas would have no place to go. At the Wanglang reserve, a bamboo die-off in the mid-1970s led to 138 panda deaths. A similar die-off could destroy Wolong's pandas.

As late as 1974, Wolong was home to 145 pandas. Twelve years later, a highly stressed panda population had been cut in half. Jianguo Liu, the lead researcher at Wolong, fears the number is still falling. "Human destruction is the most critical factor in the fate of the pandas," Liu says. If nothing is done, he adds, the time will come when pandas no longer exist in the wild.[9]

Chapter 5

An Uncertain Future

Does the giant panda have a future? Scientists believe the species has a fighting chance to escape extinction—but only a slim one. More reserves are being planned, but habitat loss is still a major worry. Poaching remains a threat, as is the danger of further bamboo die-offs. However, a worldwide network of panda lovers is working to save the bamboo bear.

The effort takes many forms. Deep in the mountains of Sichuan, out-of-work loggers restore habitat by planting

▲ *Zoos offer the giant panda protection as well as entertainment.*

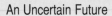

▲ Bamboo is essential to the life of a giant panda. If the bamboo on a panda reserve dies off, the local pandas will starve unless they are moved to a new habitat.

trees on bare hillsides. At the Wolong Breeding Center, a volunteer coaxes an orphan cub to eat. Schoolkids in Kansas surf the Web to watch a "panda-cam" broadcast from the Smithsonian National Zoo in Washington, D.C. In China, doctors restore a captive female's sight by removing a cataract.

When disaster strikes a panda reserve, people rally to help. The bamboo die-off of the early 1980s was one such event. Children around the globe lined up to give to "Pennies for Pandas." Japan gave nearly $250,000 for rescue teams. Scientists stepped forward to supply aid and advice.[1]

Once in a while, the drive to save the giant panda grabs headlines. In Hong Kong, action superstar Jackie Chan led the cheers at Panda Day 2000. After a choir sang a tribute

to the panda, Chan stepped forward. "The giant panda is our national treasure," he told his fans. "Everyone in Hong Kong should have a share in conserving giant pandas and their habitat."[2]

▶ Rent-a-Panda Strikes Out

The save-the-panda movement began when Su-Lin won the public's heart in the 1930s. Ever since, zoo directors have begged China to supply them with giant pandas. Zoos want pandas because they draw big crowds. Those pleas led to what some call the "Rent-a-Panda" program. When Los Angeles played host to the 1984 Olympics, China loaned two pandas to the local zoo. Over the next four years, "loaner" pandas showed up in a dozen of the world's cities.[3]

Rent-a-Panda was a moneymaker. The zoos drew overflow crowds—an increase of 750,000 paying visitors in Toronto alone. The cities enjoyed a rush of tourism, and China earned large rental fees. Called "donations for conservation," these fees averaged $100,000 per panda per month. China also received a chunk of the income from souvenir sales. Sponsors downplayed the money angle. Panda loans, they argued, put a spotlight on the plight of all endangered species.[4]

George Schaller was not impressed. He said Rent-a-Panda was marked by "greed, politics, lack of cooperation, and [a wild] scramble for pandas." Schaller worried that the stress of too much travel put the pandas' health at risk. Also on the downside, some of the loaner females missed chances to breed.[5] The critics did not stop there. They also charged that China did not spend all of the rental fees on panda conservation. After much debate, the opponents

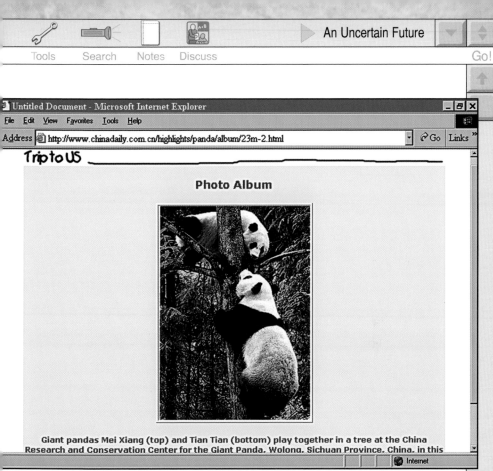

Tools Search Notes Discuss Go!

Untitled Document - Microsoft Internet Explorer

File Edit View Favorites Tools Help

Address http://www.chinadaily.com.cn/highlights/panda/album/23m-2.html Go Links

Trip to US

Photo Album

Giant pandas Mei Xiang (top) and Tian Tian (bottom) play together in a tree at the China Research and Conservation Center for the Giant Panda, Wolong, Sichuan Province, China, in this

Internet

▲ *Mei Xiang and Tian Tian were both born in the Wolong Nature Reserve. They are on a ten-year loan to the National Zoo in Washington, D.C.*

won. For the most part, the loan program came to an end in 1988.

▷ What Comes Next?

Millions of dollars have been raised for panda conservation, and more is needed. According to the American Zoo and Aquarium Association, "beyond the interests of zoos and other conservation entities is the larger issue of public concern and support. No one questions the endearing qualities of the giant panda, but unless public interest is linked to the urgent need to secure the future survival of both captive and wild

populations, this enchantment will have served little more then an entertainment function."[6]

Money is being raised. In 2002 for example, SBC Pacific Bell gave the San Diego Zoo's panda program a check for $500,000. The money was earmarked for panda research, with more to come.[7] Many smaller donations have added to the total. The Smithsonian National Zoo, for example, invites panda lovers to "adopt" its two pandas. In return for their gift, donors receive a bundle of photos and pamphlets. A Chinese Web site offers panda eco-tours as well as adoptions. In 2003, a five-day tour of the

▲ The fate of the giant panda is uncertain. People from all over the world will have to work together to save this beautiful animal.

Wolong reserve cost as little as $380 per person. The price of the deluxe tour was $670.[8]

China has tried to move farmers out of the Wolong reserve, but with little success. To resettle one village, officials built new homes farther down the mountain. The stubborn farmers refused to move. The new farmland, they said, was not fertile enough. One man came closer to explaining the real reason. "We were born here and we're staying here," he said. Another man added, "We don't see why we should move for some animals."[9] Since then, a plan has been hatched to send more village teenagers to college. After they graduate, planners expect them to find good jobs in the cities. The pressure on the reserve will ease as the village's population dwindles.[10]

▶ A Final Word

The road ahead is full of pitfalls. All too often, a step forward seems to end in a stumble. Breeding experts, for example, are keeping more captive-bred cubs alive. Out in the reserves, however, fewer cubs are seen. Money is being raised, but more is needed. China's national government is committed to the task of saving the panda. Many local officials, however, show little interest in conservation.

Panda experts Susan Lumpkin and John Seidensticker have looked long and hard at the challenge. "Science, programs, and policies won't save pandas," they write. "People will. . . . The giant panda will survive, if we let it."[11]

Perhaps zoologists Pan Wenshi and Lu Zhi should have the last word. While doing field studies in the Qinling Mountains, the two naturalists chanced upon a newborn panda. The sight of the healthy cub inspired them to name it Xi Wang, Chinese for "hope."[12] Hope is what all giant panda fans feel for the future of these shy and beautiful creatures.

This series is based on the Endangered and Threatened Wildlife list compiled by the U.S. Fish and Wildlife Service (USFWS). Each book explores an endangered or threatened animal, tells why it has become endangered or threatened, and explains the efforts being made to restore the species' population.

The United States Fish and Wildlife Service, in the Department of the Interior, and the National Marine Fisheries Service, in the Department of Commerce, share responsibility for administration of the Endangered Species Act.

In 1973, Congress took the farsighted step of creating the Endangered Species Act, widely regarded as the world's strongest and most effective wildlife conservation law. It set an ambitious goal: to reverse the alarming trend of human-caused extinction that threatened the ecosystems we all share.

The complete list of Endangered and Threatened Wildlife and Plants can be found at **http://endangered.fws.gov/wildlife.html#Species**

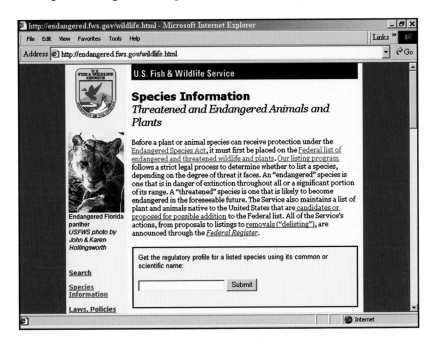

Chapter 1. *Ailuropoda melanoleuca*

1. Susan Lumpkin and John Seidensticker, *Smithsonian Book of Giant Pandas* (Washington, D.C.: Smithsonian Institution Press, 2002), pp. 16–17.

2. Judith Janda Presnall, *The Giant Panda* (San Diego, Calif.: Lucent Books, 1998), p. 54.

3. "A Tibetan Panda Myth," n.d., <http://www.geocities.com/RainForest/3019/myth.html> July 21, 2002.

4. George Schaller, *The Last Panda* (Chicago: University of Chicago Press, 1993), p. 261.

5. "Panda Facts," *Wanglang Nature Reserve*, January 22, 2001, <http://www.slack.net/~rd/wanglang/panda_facts.htm> (September 5, 2003).

6. Quoted in Schaller, p. 267.

Chapter 2. A Lonely Life on a Bamboo Mountain

1. George Schaller, The Last Panda (Chicago: University of Chicago Press, 1993), p. 1.

2. "Giant Pandas: the Bear Facts," n.d., <http://pandas.si.edu/facts/bearfacts.htm>, July 21, 2002.

3. "Panda Facts," *Wanglang Nature Reserve*, January 22, 2001, <http://www.slack.net/~rd/wanglang/panda_facts.htm> (September 5, 2003).

4. Susan Lumpkin and John Seidensticker, *Smithsonian Book of Giant Pandas* (Washington, D.C.: Smithsonian Institution Press, 2002), pp. 64–68.

5. Ibid., p. 75.

6. Chris Catton, *Pandas* (New York: Facts on File Publications, 1990), p. 28.

7. "Panda Facts," *Wanglang Nature Reserve*.

8. Devra G. Kleiman, "Giant Pandas: Bamboo Bears," 1992, <http://pandas.si.edu/facts/kleimanbamboobears.htm> July 21, 2002.

9. Schaller, pp. 65–66.

10. Ibid., pp. 82–83.

11. Presnall, pp. 21–22.

Chapter 3. Threats to the Giant Panda's Survival

1. George Schaller, *The Last Panda* (Chicago: University of Chicago Press, 1993), pp. 126–129.

2. Barbara Radcliffe Rogers, *Giant Pandas* (New York: Mallard Press, 1990), pp. 74, 106.

3. Susan Lumpkin, "Giant Pandas and Bamboo," ZooGoer, 1992, <http://pandas.si.edu/facts/giantpanda&bamboo.htm>, July 21, 2002.

4. Schaller, p. 224.

5. G. B. Schaller, as quoted by Paul Massicot, "*Ailuropoda melanoleuca*," Animal Info, 1999–2003, <http://www.animalinfo.org/species/carnivor/ailumela.htm> (September 5, 2003).

6. Schaller, p. 227.

7. Chris Catton, *Pandas* (New York: Facts on File Publications, 1990), p. 118.

8. Ibid.

9. Ibid., p. 109.

10. Rogers, p. 30.

11. Susan Lumpkin and John Seidensticker, *Smithsonian Book of Giant Pandas* (Washington, D.C.: Smithsonian Institution Press, 2002), pp. 6–7.

12. "Panda-Friendly Forests Disappearing," April 6, 2002, <http://www.hypography.com/article.cfm/30678.html> July 24, 2002.

13. "Experts Seek Ways to Avoid Inbreeding Among Pandas," *Embassy of the People's Republic of China in the Kingdom of Belgium*, January 2002, <http://www.chinaembassy-org.be/eng/23358.html> (September 5, 2003).

14. Quoted in Schaller, p. 151.

Chapter 4. Save the Giant Panda!

1. Chris Catton, *Pandas* (New York: Facts on File Publications, 1990), pp. 7–8.

2. Public Broadcasting Service, "The Panda Baby," *Nature*, n.d., <http://www.pbs.org/wnet/nature/panda/cub.html> (September 5, 2003).

3. "Conservation," Panda, n.d., <http://www.iwec.org/Kits/panda1.htm> July 22, 2002.

4. "Fourth Annual State of the Panda at San Diego Zoo," Panda Facts—Helping the Panda, n.d., <http://www.sandiegozoo.org/special/pandas/ask/sop2002.html> July 21, 2002.

5. Ibid.

6. "Panda Gigante," *Zoo Aquarium de la Casa de Campo de Madrid*, n.d., <http://carol.wns.uva.nl/~jonk/pandas/madrid.html> (September 5, 2003).

7. "Panda Breeding & Research Centers," WorldWild Tours Journal from China, n.d., <http://www.sandiegozoo.org/wildideas/worldwild/cause_journal_china3.html> July 24, 2002.

8. George Schaller, *The Last Panda* (Chicago: University of Chicago Press, 1993), p. 228.

9. "Study: China Failing to Protect Panda Preserve," *CNN.com—Sci-Tech*, April 5, 2001, <http://www.cnn.com/2001/TECH/science/04/05/panda.endangered/> July 24, 2002.

Chapter 5. An Uncertain Future

1. Chris Catton, *Pandas* (New York: Facts on File Publications, 1990), p. 77.

2. "Panda Day 2000," Hong Kong Society for Panda Conservation, n.d., <http://www.hkpanda.org/public_pandaday.htm> July 22, 2002.

3. Audra Ang, "Critics Question China's Worldwide Panda Profit," *The Age*, April 5, 2003, <http://www.theage.com.au/articles/2003/04/04/1048962931531.html> (September 5, 2003).

4. Ibid.

5. George Schaller, *The Last Panda* (Chicago: University of Chicago Press, 1993), p. 236.

6. Dr. Donald G. Lindburg, coordinator, "Giant Panda," *American Zoo and Aquarium Association*, 2002, <http://www.giantpandaonline.org> (September 5, 2003).

7. "Fourth Annual State of the Panda at San Diego Zoo," Panda Facts—Helping the Panda, n.d., <http://www.sandiegozoo.org/special/pandas/ask/sop2002.html> July 21, 2002.

8. "Wolong Reserve & Chengdu Base Tour," *Giant Panda Tour*, n.d., <http://www.4panda.com/panda/index.htm> September 14, 2002.

9. Presnall, pp. 74–75.

10. "Panda-Friendly Forests Disappearing," April 6, 2002, <http://www.hypography.com/article.cfm/30678.html> July 24, 2002.

11. Susan Lumpkin and John Seidensticker, *Smithsonian Book of Giant Pandas* (Washington, D.C.: Smithsonian Institution Press, 2002), p. 186.

12. "The Giant Panda Photo Gallery," *World Wildlife Fund*, n.d., <http://www.panda.org/photogallery/gallery.cfm?uGalleryID=43&uImageID=147> (September 5, 2003).

Angel, Heather. *Pandas*. Stillwater, Minn.: Voyageur Press, 1998.

Catton, Chris. *Pandas*. New York: Facts on File Publications, 1990.

Dudley, Karen. *Giant Pandas*. Austin, Tex.: Raintree Steck-Vaughn Publishers, 1997.

Leeson, Pat and Tom Leeson. *Panda*. Woodbridge, Conn.: Blackbirch Press, 2000.

Lumpkin, Susan and John Seidensticker. *Smithsonian Book of Giant Pandas*. Washington, D.C.: Smithsonian Institution Press, 2002.

Penny, Malcolm. *Giant Panda: Habitats, Life Cycles, Food Chains, Threats*. Austin, Tex.: Raintree Steck-Vaughn Publishers, 2000.

Preiss, Byron and Gao Xueyu. *The Secret World of Pandas*. New York: Harry N. Abrams, Publishers, 1990.

Presnall, Judith Janda. *The Giant Panda*. San Diego, Calif.: Lucent Books, 1998.

Rogers, Barbara Radcliffe. *Giant Pandas*. New York: Mallard Press, 1990.

Schaller, George B., Hu Jinchu, Pan Wenshi, and Zhu Jing. *The Last Panda*. Chicago: The University of Chicago Press, 1993.